Keep Yourself Safe on the Internet

Keep Your Plans Private

Nancy Greenwood

PowerKiDS press
New York

Published in 2018 by The Rosen Publishing Group, Inc.
29 East 21st Street, New York, NY 10010

Editor: Greg Roza
Book Design: Rachel Rising
Interior Layout: Michael Flynn

Photo Credits: Cover JGI/Jamie Grill/Blend Images/Getty Images; cover, pp. 3–4, 6, 8, 10, 12, 14, 16, 18, 20, 22–24 (background) Creative Mood/Shutterstock.com; p. 5 wavebreakmedia/Shutterstock.com; pp. 7, 19 Monkey Business Images/Shutterstock.com; p. 9 Stuart Monk/Shutterstock.com; p. 11 sirtravelalot/Shutterstock.com; p. 13 Prostock-studio/Shutterstock.com; p. 15 Thomas Barwick/Iconica/Getty Images; p. 17 Images by Christina Kilgour/Moment Select/Getty Images; p. 21 Jordan Siemens/DigitalVision/Getty Images; p. 22 Africa Studio/Shutterstock.com.

Cataloging-in-Publication Data

Names: Greenwood, Nancy.
Title: Keep your plans private / Nancy Greenwood.
Description: New York : PowerKids Press, 2018. | Series: Keep yourself safe on the internet | Includes index.
Identifiers: ISBN 9781538325797 (pbk.) | ISBN 9781538325070 (library bound) | ISBN 9781538325803 (6 pack)
Subjects: LCSH: Internet--Safety measures--Juvenile literature.| Internet and children--Juvenile literature.
Classification: LCC HQ784.I58 G74 2018 | DDC 025.04'0289--dc23

Manufactured in the United States of America

CPSIA Compliance Information: Batch #BW18PK For further information contact Rosen Publishing, New York, New York at 1-800-237-9932.

Contents

Safety First

Do you like going online? You can play games and do homework. You can **communicate** with friends on the Internet. You have to make sure you're staying safe online.

Plans are things you're going to do. Plans can be things you do every day, or things you only do some days. Your plans are **private**. Don't share your plans online.

Are you going to school today? Will you walk or take the bus? Are you going to soccer practice after school? These are all plans.

SCHOOL BUS

Plans tell people where you're going to be. Your parents and teachers need to know your plans to keep you safe. Strangers, or people you don't know, shouldn't know your plans.

Plans Are Private

A stranger could try to talk to you online. They might ask you about your plans. Don't tell them. Tell a trusted adult if this happens.

Many adults want you to be safe. A trusted adult may be a teacher, coach, or parent. They can help you if a stranger online is asking about your plans.

Ask for Help

Some **websites** let you post about your plans for your friends to see. Sometimes other people can see these posts. Don't post your plans online. A stranger could see them, even if you thought only your friends could see them.

You can talk to your friends online. An adult can help you find **secure** websites to use. Some websites are safe and won't share your plans with others.

If a stranger knows your plans, they could find your home. They could follow you. That would be scary. That's why it's important to keep your plans private.

Always keep your plans private. Never share them online. That will help you stay safe on and off the Internet!

Glossary

communicate: To share thoughts and feelings with other people.

private: Not meant for other people to know.

secure: Safe from danger.

website: A page on the Internet.

Index

Websites

Due to the changing nature of Internet links, PowerKids Press has developed an online list of websites related to the subject of this book. This site is updated regularly. Please use this link to access the list: www.powerkidslinks.com/kysi/plans